MW00952955

# Move to Italy...Why Not?

## A Complete Guide For Wannabe Expats

**By The Expat Homes Team**

**Copyright 2022. All rights reserved.**

# Table of contents

## Introduction

Italy is a beautiful country with a rich history that quite literally has something for everyone. Whether you like skiing in the Alps, sipping wine in Tuscany, high fashion in Milan or the hustle and bustle of Rome, there is no shortage of amazing experiences in Italy.

Architecture, art, food and music are as much a part of Italian culture as baseball and apple pie are to the U.S., or maple syrup and hockey are to Canada. Honoring and embracing the culture in Italy is a way of life for Italians and expats alike.

As one of the most popular tourist destinations in the world, it's no wonder that Italy is also a popular relocation destination for expats. Many people dream of moving to Italy to start a new life, or as a reward to themselves for their retirement.

The slow pace of life, relatively low cost of living and high-quality healthcare make Italy especially desirable for retirees.

Because of this, Italy has created a few specific visas designed for retirees who wish to spend the rest of their lives in Italy.

Moving to Italy will take some money. Before they allow you to stay longer than the time allowed on a tourist visa, you'll need to prove that you have ample funds (visa by investment) or ample income from your investments (steady dividends well above the minimum income threshold). There are a few exceptions to this covered in the immigration chapter, but it's not as easy for a foreigner to move to Italy as it would be for someone from Iowa to move to Florida.

There are twenty regions in Italy and they are all very different. Deciding where in Italy to call home deserves some serious consideration, especially when it comes to the big items of importance like access to healthcare, climate, transportation (local and international) and taxes.

Northern Italy and Southern Italy are very different places with very different cultures. Making several trips to Italy to explore the different regions is highly recommended before you start moving forward with an eventual relocation to Italy. (Difficult advice to swallow...I know).

## Some useful things to know

Many Italians do not speak English. Westerners (specifically from the U.S. and Canada) are sometimes shocked to find that not everyone in the world speaks English!

You will want to learn Italian as quickly as possible if you don't already speak it. There are also regional dialects in the Italian language, so be prepared for some inconsistencies as you travel about the country. The generic language acquisition apps are great to get started, but some lessons from a local, native Italian speaker will serve you well once you get settled.

Bureaucracy and red tape are part of life in Italy. It takes a bit of patience and perseverance  to navigate things that are seemingly simple, like obtaining a driver's license or paying your taxes. Brace yourself for delays and maybe a little frustration as you learn to navigate the systems in place in Italy.

For your own sanity, I discourage you from asking questions such as, "Why do they do it that way when this other way would be so much easier?" The bureaucracy and red tape are unlikely to change. You will be much happier if you accept them as a way of life and learn to live with them.

Family and community are important parts of Italian life as well. You will see this manifest in many ways, such as a family business being passed from generation to generation, or extended families living under the same roof. There are frequent family gatherings among extended family members in Italy and the children are taught from a young age about the importance of family ties.

The primary religion in Italy is Roman Catholicism, which is no surprise. The Vatican is considered the international hub for Catholicism and is located in the center of Rome. Roughly 75% of the country is Catholic or Christian, and roughly 20% is Muslim, with other religions making up the difference.

Traditionally, there were clearly defined gender roles in Italian society. Men were considered the head of the household, while women were considered the soul. Today, Italian women are some of the most liberated in all of Europe.

Some of the etiquette in Italy can be surprising if you're not prepared for it. The ideas of personal space and queueing in a line are non-existent in many parts of the country. Young women are expected to defer to older men and not contradict what is said (although older women aren't expected to follow that particular rule). Kissing, hugging and touching are all part of daily life among friends and even strangers. Also, elders are treated with the utmost respect by everyone.

Dressing well is important to Italians. Taking pride in one's appearance is a part of the culture. Even for quick trips to the store, you won't see an Italian wearing flip-flops and sweatpants—they will be dressed with some attention paid to proper fashion. The focus on fashion is natural given that Milan is considered one of the most important fashion capitals in the world.

## Immigration and visas

Every country in the world has restrictions and bureaucracy when it comes to immigration laws. The countries who want to encourage immigration make it easy and keep the bureaucracy to a minimum. The countries who want to discourage immigration pile on the monetary requirements and red tape.

Italy has reasonable requirements if you want to move there, such as proof of income, health insurance and a background check. The requirements are reasonable, although most would say they're on the difficult end of the spectrum when all things are considered. Heavy bureaucracy is "just the way they do things" in Italy and that includes the immigration process.

To make it even more fun, it is entirely possible you will get different answers about the paperwork and other requirements for your application from different consulates! Consulates are staffed with bureaucrats, after all, and you know how that works everywhere in the world.

Whether you are planning a permanent or seasonal relocation to Italy, you will want to know the laws and how they apply to you.

**Schengen Area**

The Schengen Area in Europe consists of 26 countries. They have all agreed to abolish border control and passport checks with the other member countries. Anyone who has a visa to one of the member countries can travel freely to any of the other member countries. Here's the full list:

Austria
Belgium
Czech Republic
Denmark
Estonia
Finland
France
Germany
Greece
Hungary
Iceland
Italy
Latvia
Liechtenstein
Lithuania
Luxembourg
Malta
Netherlands

Norway

Poland

Portugal

Slovakia

Slovenia

Spain

Sweden

Switzerland

As of early 2020, there are also five countries petitioning to join Schengen—Ireland, Bulgaria, Croatia, Cyprus and Romania.

All Schengen members are part of the EU, but not all EU countries are part of Schengen. As you can see, Italy and its neighbors are all Schengen members.

Travel to the Schengen zone is limited to 90 days out of every 180 days for anyone who does not have a proper residency visa for one of the Schengen countries. The 90 day limit is a rolling number, so you can't leave for a day to a non-Schengen country and return to Schengen to restart the clock. Once you have spent 90 days in Schengen, you will need to leave for at least 90 days before you can legally return.

Also, be very careful about trying to game the system here. They pay attention at the borders when you enter and exit. If you are consistently doing something like spending 87 days in Italy, leaving for three months, then spending another 85 days, etc., it will look suspicious and you may get flagged. And by "flagged," I mean labeled an illegal immigrant and banned from the country (and the rest of Schengen). It's not worth trying to get away with it. Either go through the process and become an official resident, or get comfortable keeping your status as a tourist.

Once you have a proper residency permit that shows you live in a Schengen country, your travel throughout Schengen will not be restricted.

### Residency and citizenship options

Fairly recent Italian ancestry or marriage to an Italian citizen can make the immigration process a little easier for you (but still not "easy"). Without those exceptions, you will need to follow the rules through one of the other immigration avenues like everyone else.

## Student visa

This is a great option for those who are non-permanent extended stay in Italy. You can qualify if you are part of your university's study abroad program or if you are enrolling in an Italian university.

You ALSO qualify if you are taking a single course about Italian history or culture, or are in a professional training or internship program. Maybe you want to learn how to make wine and find a winery who will teach you. Maybe you want to learn how to cook authentic Italian meals and find a chef who will teach you. There are some interesting possibilities here. It's important to note that if you are working when you have a student visa, you are limited to 20 hours per week.

It is possible to have a student visa extended for a few years if you can justify the reason (continued study, continued professional training, etc.). It is also possible to use a student visa to build relationships and experience, and secure a full-time job with a company who will sponsor you for a proper work visa so you can stay in Italy indefinitely.

### Work visa

Getting a work visa is almost impossible unless you have special skills and a working relationship with a multi-national company who is willing to manage your relocation and visa process there. Italy protects the available jobs and wants them to go to Italians. One exception to this is the student visa approach outlined above.

The company is responsible for proving that people with your skills are not available at the local level to justify the need to hire you and bring you over. They will also have to do all the work to get you a permit, which will be sent to you so you can apply for a visa at the Italian consulate in your home country before arriving.

Working remotely for a company located outside of Italy is not an option for obtaining a work visa.

### Family visa

This visa is when an entire family enters Italy at the same time and plans to leave at the same time. It only applies if there is a qualifying person in the family who has legitimate residency of some kind. Be prepared to prove your relationship to the qualifying person, relationship to all the family members traveling together and the other usual travel documents required to enter Italy.

**Elective Residency Visa (ERV)**

This visa is great if you can afford to live in Italy without needing to work. Doing work of any kind (including remote, online work) is prohibited with this visa. People with substantial cash, investments or retirement pensions are the ones who fit well with this visa.

The financial requirements for the ERV are straightforward. The minimum monthly income for an individual from pensions, interest, dividends, etc. must be a minimum of €2,596.60 (or roughly USD $40,000 annually). Why they didn't just round it up to the nearest euro to make it an even number is beyond me. The Italian government likes to see much MORE than the minimum amount required, so think twice about applying if your income is cutting it close.

The documentation you need to provide includes original bank statements (not copies) and a letter from your bank stating the current funds available, type of accounts and the monthly earnings. They want to see your funds producing income, not just drawing down the principal amount you have on deposit with the bank. If you have other sources of income such as royalties, rental income from investment properties or regular dividends from other investments, bring all the documentation you have about those sources as well.

You will also need a cover letter that explains your reasons for wanting to be in Italy for the length of the visa. It doesn't have to be elaborate, but you should take care to explain anything about your situation that might not seem straightforward to a bureaucrat. You will need to include copies of birth certificates and/or marriage certificates for everyone in your family who will be included with the visa.

In addition to the financial requirements, you will also have to provide proof of health insurance with a minimum coverage threshold and proof of residency in Italy. Travelers insurance is acceptable for this purpose. The insurance policy will have to be translated into Italian and stamped by the Italian embassy in your home country in order for it to be acceptable for the visa.

Proof of residency will be required with the application as well (a rental contract or a deed to a property you already own). This can be a tricky one. It seems like a chicken and egg problem, doesn't it? How am I supposed to get a landlord to rent me an apartment before I'm an official resident? How can I get official residency without an apartment?

These are the recommended steps for establishing a place to live. Keep in mind that rental contracts can be cancelled within six months of being signed if you are unable to obtain a proper visa. Be sure to explain your situation to your agent and landlord when discussing the lease. Italian landlords understand bureaucracy and red tape very well, so you want to be sure they know what's happening and why.

*(You can skip this part if you already own a property, or have a notarized affidavit of an invitation to stay with a legal Italian resident.)*

1.  Make a trip to Italy as a tourist. Your main task for this trip (besides eating and drinking all the Italian things) is to secure a rental contract for an apartment. You have 90 days to do this per Schengen rules, but it shouldn't take you that long.

2. You will need a *codice fiscale* in order to sign the rental contract, which is free and relatively painless to obtain (see the chapter on housing for details).
3. Register the rental contract with the appropriate local government office.
4. Return to your home country with your rental contract.
5. Apply for the ERV with all of your documentation.
6. Get approved, pick up your visa and move to Italy.
7. Register for the long-term permission to stay in Italy at the local police station within **eight business days** of your arrival (the *permesso di soggiorno*).

Please keep in mind they will not accept hotels, multiple dwellings (like, moving to a new address every few weeks) or Airbnb-type arrangements as a proof of residence. You'll have to pick one place and commit to it.

**Visa by investment**

You can obtain permanent residency in Italy by making a large investment. Your options:

€500,000 invested in an "innovative" startup company

€1,000,000 donation to an Italian charity or philanthropic cause

€1,000,000 loan to an Italian limited company

€2,000,000 invested in Italian government bonds

**Type D visa**

There is a small business or "startup" visa called Type D. It is the closest thing to a self-employment or freelancer visa that exists in Italy. You will need to have sufficient funds to cover yourself and any family members, and jump through quite a few hoops with the local chamber of commerce in the area where you live. (Note: The chamber of commerce in Italy is a government entity and is not related to the organization with the same name that exists as a private business club in the US.)

They are stingy with the Type D visas because claiming you are "working on a startup" is easy to abuse for visas if they just take your word for it. Your business plan must be solid and you will want an Italian lawyer and an Italian accountant who specialize in Type D visas to help you prepare everything you need. Bonus points if your business provides a service or product that caters to the Italian market.

**How to become an Italian citizen**

The easiest way to become an Italian citizen is to be born in Italy to Italian parents! Too late for that one? Okay, keep reading.

Having Italian ancestry or marrying an Italian citizen are two ways to obtain Italian citizenship.

Another option to consider is if you have lineage to any other EU country and can obtain citizenship via ancestry there. Once you are a citizen in another EU country, you will have the freedom to move around the EU (including Italy!) as you see fit without restrictions. Obviously, this opens the door to some other legal and tax complexities, but it's an option for some who don't have Italian blood or an Italian spouse.

Some countries allow dual citizenship and others simply don't "recognize" dual citizenship (you're a citizen of their country in their eyes and anything you do with additional citizenship outside of that relationship is not of their concern).

Check with your home country to find out if it's possible for you. Italy has no restrictions on dual citizenship.

## Citizenship by ancestry ("Jure Sanguinis")

In 1912, Italian citizenship law declared that only men could pass Italian citizenship to their children. Your bloodline had to be traced to an Italian male in order to qualify.

In 1948, the law changed to allow women to pass Italian citizenship through their bloodlines as well. Anyone born to an Italian woman after 1948 would also qualify for citizenship.

For those born to an Italian woman before 1948, citizenship is still possible but it requires some legal work. You'll have to provide the necessary birth records (Italian and home country) proving your bloodline, naturalization papers showing where your ancestor immigrated and hire a lawyer to file a petition at the *one* court in Rome that hears those cases for all of Italy.

Fair warning #1: It can take several years for your case to be heard in court (although your lawyer can attend on your behalf so you don't need to make a special trip).

Fair warning #2: Obtaining original birth records from your ancestors' towns in Italy can be a daunting task. It will take time, patience and perseverance. The good news is you can go as far back in your ancestry as you need to in order to prove your Italian ancestry. Of course, the further back you have to go, the harder it will be to find the required documentation.

**Citizenship by marriage ("Jure Matrimonii")**

Citizenship by marriage or civil union is available after two years for couples who were living in Italy, and three years for couples who were living outside of Italy. The waiting time is shortened for those who have children under age 18 (one year for couples living in Italy and 18 months for couples outside of Italy). The children can be biological or adopted.

There is an extra Italian language proficiency requirement for those seeking citizenship by marriage. The non-Italian partner must be proficient in Italian at the B1 level from an institution approved by the Italian Ministry of Education or the Ministry of Foreign Affairs.

One final requirement for citizenship marriage is the registration of the marriage or civil union with the local Italian consulate, or registration with AIRE if living outside of Italy.

AIRE is the registry of Italian citizens living abroad that is managed by the Italian government to keep tabs on Italian citizens who are living outside of Italy. AIRE registration is important for other reasons as well, such as voting from afar and regular consulate services.

### Citizenship through naturalization

Becoming a naturalized citizen of Italy can happen in a few different ways. A spouse of an Italian citizen can apply after ten years of living in Italy assuming they can prove ample financial resources and have no criminal record.

People without proof of citizenship elsewhere (such as refugees who landed on Italian shores with no documentation) can start the naturalization process after five years. EU citizens have a four-year waiting period after moving to Italy before they can apply for naturalization.

One last avenue is if the applicant was born in Italy and their grandparents were Italian citizens. In that scenario, the waiting time is only three years.

# Transportation

There are a few primary modes of transportation in Italy. In the big cities, it's usually easy to get around just fine on foot. In rural areas, you will want to have some other options available to you.

The train system (*Trenitalia*) in Italy is very good. It is a state-run system that provides transportation to most of the country. Tickets can be booked up to two months in advance, and can be purchased online or through the Trenitalia smart phone apps. Keep in mind that some routes are busy and will be fully booked, so it pays to plan in advance. Train tickets are relatively inexpensive compared to other European countries.

The bus network in Italy is also substantial. Buses are the preferred mode of transportation when traveling to and from smaller cities and villages that are not serviced by the train system, in addition to getting around the larger cities.

The ferry system provides some options for transportation in the coastal regions. There are ferries to the Italian islands, in addition to various international locations. Some of the popular international destinations are Croatia, France, Greece and Malta. It is always advisable to buy tickets well in advance of your trip.

There are a few dozen airports in Italy that run commercial flights. Most of the time, it's easiest to arrive at one of the major airports in Rome, Milan or Venice and then figure out alternative transportation options from there. The large, urban hubs have easy access to bus and train routes from the airports to make life easier for you.

For those who enjoy having their own car, there are a few things to note. Some countries have agreements with each other that allow for "swapping" of drivers' licenses (this is not an option if you are from the U.S.). Your current driver's license will be valid for up to one year after you relocate to Italy.

**Driver's license**

As with many things in Italy, there is some hefty bureaucracy when it comes to getting a driver's license.

It is possible to go straight to the *Ufficio Motorizzazione Civile* (the Italian version of the DMV) to take the driver's test. Most people prefer to attend a school because both the written and driving portions of the test at Ufficio

Motorizzazione Civile are difficult. The private schools make it easier for you to pass the first time and get you familiar with the vocabulary and structure of the questions on the exam. You can expect cumbersome paperwork and long wait times as with any government office.

If you are bringing a personal car with you from somewhere in the EU, be sure to bring all the documentation showing recent inspections and proper registration. It will make your life much easier when you register the car in Italy. If you are bringing a car from outside the EU, you will have to go through a few extra steps with the Ufficio Motorizzazione Civile to be sure it meets the property environmental and safety requirements.

## Housing

You may have heard about places in Italy where the government will sell you an old house or even an entire castle for one euro. It's not a joke!

The catch is that you have to renovate the property in the next year or two and put it into use as a hotel, bed & breakfast, or something similar.

The government is willing to do this for several reasons. They are interested in attracting capital from outside of Italy to invest in real estate, and they are interested in bringing some of the ancient villages back to life to alleviate overcrowding from tourists in the popular vacation spots. There are plenty of awesome places in Italy outside of the tourist zones and the government wants more people to experience those places in style.

A "one euro" house can be a great deal for the right person. With that said, I think it's safe to assume most people in the world should probably not be shopping for a one euro house. The complexities of permits, managing contractors and construction challenges make it a complicated task.

Some things to consider: Are you fluent in written and spoken Italian? Do you know any contractors in town? Have you ever managed a construction project before? Did you know there's no Home Depot? Who is going to run the hotel or B&B once it's completed?

There's also the matter of having enough cash to cover your living expenses AND all the renovation costs for a year or two while the work is being completed. (You will have to provide banking documentation that you have the funds to complete the work before they'll approve your one euro purchase).

If you have the money and the construction experience, I certainly don't want to discourage you from checking on the one euro property options. They can be great situations for ambitious people who are looking for a big project. Most people will be happier buying a property that requires less time, less work and less money to be livable.

Once you get outside the major metropolitan areas, there are PLENTY of inexpensive houses for sale. However, just because a house is inexpensive doesn't necessarily make it a good idea to buy it.

Many of the least expensive houses were built hundreds of years ago and they have fallen into a state of disrepair. Others may have been renovated or partially renovated at some point (or renovated several times in their existence), but they need some serious attention again to bring them up to modern standards.

**Renting**

Most Italians live in apartments. For the majority of people moving to Italy, they will also be living in apartments. The regular pattern for those relocating to Italy is to find short-term housing or medium-term housing (through places like Airbnb) to get started.

Before you dive into the long-term rental game, there are some things you should know.

The leasing situation in Italy has some key differences from other parts of the world. The rental paperwork can be daunting and there are some uncommon considerations such as taxes. That's right, there are taxes that have to be paid as a renter.

Once you have done your research and narrowed your search to a few different neighborhoods, it's wise to enlist the help of a local rental agent. Agents help with the entire process, from finding a suitable place for you to understanding the paperwork and processes that will likely be foreign to you.

Fees for renting through an agency are paid by the renter. For long-term and short-term rentals, you can expect to pay the equivalent of one month's rent. There are usually no additional fees for rentals with a duration under 30 days.

An understanding of the different types of rental agreements is important when you begin your search.

One type of lease is a *free market contract* (or contratto di libero mercato). This type of agreement lasts for four years, with the option to renew for another four years. The slang you may see in advertising is "4 + 4."

The second type of lease is a *mutually agreed contract* (contratti concertati), which is a bit more flexible with the terms between landlord and tenant. The term is for three years with a two-year renewal option ("3 + 2"), or sometimes four years with a two-year renewal option ("4 + 2").

A third type of lease is a *transitory contract* (uso transitorio) which lasts between one month and eighteen months. These are common in areas where businesses are hiring temporary or contract workers on a regular basis.

There are also student rentals (uso studenti universitari) which have a term of anywhere from six months to three years. Student rental contracts are only allowed in municipalities where there is a university, or where there is a university in the neighboring municipality.

The deposit amount is usually the equivalent of 2-4 month's rent, depending on the condition of the property. Nicer places will require larger deposits. You should ALWAYS ask for a separate written receipt for the deposit amount and have a clear understanding of how and when it will be returned to you when you leave.

The rental cost and the deposit amount are sometimes negotiable. It depends mostly on market conditions, just like most other places in the world.

IMPORTANT: There are some scams running on a regular basis in every major city in the world. They are especially prevalent in places that are popular with foreigners, such as Italy.

One common scam is when someone tries to get you to leave a deposit on a place before you have seen it. People looking at housing from a distance are especially susceptible to this one.

The usual routine is the scammer advertises a place for rent that has beautiful photos, it's in a popular part of town and it is very inexpensive. When you see it, you contact the scammer because you don't want to lose this deal that is too good to be true. (It's too good to be true because it doesn't exist in the first place.) The scammer persuades you to wire money as a deposit to "hold" the apartment until you can get there. Your money is gone as soon as you wire it.

Another common scam is when a place is advertised for rent by someone who is not authorized to offer it for rent. The differences with this scam are that the apartment actually DOES exist and you may have seen it in-person. This scam can be run by someone renting a place for a short-term who pretends to be the landlord, or by relatives of the actual landlord who are not authorized to offer it for rent or sign any legal documents on behalf of the landlord.

One way to guard against both of these scams is to demand to see proof of ownership before you sign a lease or hand over any money. A legitimate landlord will provide you with a lease to review along with documentation that proves their ownership. Most rental agencies will help you with this, but you should do your own review of the documentation just in case.

Another way to avoid being scammed is to never sign anything or leave a deposit for a place you haven't seen in-person. This advice might seem obvious, but the scammers have been running this scam for many years and they would have stopped long ago if it didn't work some of the time.

There will be a stated efficiency rating for the unit as well. This is a standard requirement anywhere in the European Union when properties are put for sale or for rent. The ratings are used to standardize the communication about energy efficiency across the EU.

Today, there are ten ratings on the scale, which are A4, A3, A2, A1, B, C, D, E, F and G, with A4 being the most efficient and G the least efficient. That scale went into effect in 2015 across the EU.

The energy efficiency certificates that were issued until the fall of 2015 are still in use in some places because they are good for ten years. You may also see the previous scale, which is similar, but a little different. The previous ratings were A+, A, B, C, D, E, F and G.

Different appliances have different rating systems, but they are all on the same basic scale. A quick glance at the labels on the appliances will give you an idea of the level of efficiency. Older appliances are generally less energy efficient, so it's important to check any appliances that seem a bit dated for their ratings if you are concerned about your energy costs.

Electricity can be very expensive in Italy, so you'll want to be aware of the efficiency ratings of any property you rent. Having the air conditioning running all the time in the summer can make your electricity bill soar.

Another item to consider that you might not think to consider ahead of time is the internet. Some buildings (and entire villages!) are not wired for the internet, and some units have restrictions on whether or not the internet can be run into them. If you are like me and the internet is important for a happy life, this is an important thing to know.

It is critical to have a complete understanding of the rental paperwork. You will want to have a native Italian speaker read it and explain it to you. It's worth it to pay a few euros for someone to do this for you. Some of the items in the contract might seem strange, so don't be afraid to ask questions.

One unique clause you might see relates to the numbers published by the National Institute of Statistics (ISTAT). ISTAT publishes national statistics on the Italian economy and consumer indices. An ISTAT clause in your contract could allow your landlord to raise the rent once a year if the economic numbers support the increase.

As a tenant, you will usually be responsible for the maintenance and repair of all the appliances in the unit. You will also have to arrange and pay for regular servicing of things like the hot water heater, any heating or air conditioning systems and exterior doors and windows. It is also common to have a painting clause in the contract that will make you responsible for painting yourself or paying a painting contractor when your lease terminates.

It's a good idea to ask the owner or agency for a copy of all the expenses from the past year so you can see what to expect regarding expenses. It won't be exactly what you can expect to pay, but it's helpful to get the full picture.

Other components of the rental contracts will seem familiar. Things like an early termination clause and regular wear-and-tear can be expected. Good practices like taking photos and videos upon moving-in and getting all agreements with your landlord in writing are universal. It's a good policy to expect the best and prepare for the worst. When everything is in writing, it's much easier to manage any future disagreements.

When everything is agreed, it is also important to register your rental contract with the local municipality. This will cost a little money, but it's not a big expense and the amount varies from place to place. The registration cost should be shared equally between the renter and the landlord and will probably require a trip to the local government building.

**Buying property in Italy**

The dream of owning a house in the Italian countryside is an unsurprisingly popular one. With the idyllic landscape, the centuries of tradition, the world-class food and wine, and the high quality of life make Italy a desirable destination for just about anyone.

Not everyone is eligible to buy property in Italy, though.

The people who can buy property in Italy without any restrictions are Italian citizens, European Union citizens, European Economic Area citizens (Iceland, Liechtenstein and Norway) or refugees without any citizenship who have lived in Italy for at least three years.

For foreigners living in Italy who do not fit any of the above qualifications, it is still possible to buy property with a valid residence card. The residence card must be issued for one of the following reasons:

- Possession of a valid European Commission residence card (available after living in an EU country for at least five years)
- Study at an accredited school
- Valid family reasons
- Italian business ownership
- Self-employment in Italy
- Official humanitarian work

The third way it is legally possible for foreigners to buy property in Italy is due to a reciprocal agreement between Italy and the foreigners' home countries. Basically, you are allowed to buy property in Italy if your country allows Italians to buy property in your country.

**The purchase process**

The property search process is similar to what you experience in other countries. There are websites listing properties in different areas, and it's always wise to work with an agent you trust. In the areas where it's common for foreigners to buy Italian properties, you should be able to find English-speaking agents. Local agents are extra valuable because they may know about properties for sale that aren't publicly listed. This website is a good place to start: Espatriati

You'll need to have your *codice fiscale* (Italian identification number) and an Italian bank account before you write an offer on a property you like. You may also want an Italian lawyer/solicitor to guide you through the process along with the help of your agent.

The formal purchase offer is called a *proposta d'acquisito,* and it becomes a legally-binding document as soon as a seller accepts your offer. Once the seller accepts your offer, the contract is called a *compromesso* (a preliminary contract). It has to be registered with the local government within 20 days in order to be considered valid, which usually costs a few hundred euro.

After the paperwork is official, you will leave a deposit (10% of the purchase price is typical). You will be subject to a penalty of double the deposit amount if you change your mind and cancel the deal after that point.

Notaries manage the closing process in Italy instead of attorneys, escrow companies or title insurance companies. The buyer is responsible for paying the notaries' fees.

Once all the documentation is in order, the notary will set a closing date. The buyer, seller, notary and any agents attend the closing. All of the contact paperwork will be in Italian, so be sure you have a translator with you (like your agent or lawyer). The property is yours once the money changes hands and the paperwork is complete!

## The renovation process (for brave expats only)

The reality TV shows about renovating houses make it look easy. When it comes to renovating properties in Italy, it's a little different.

The laws about renovations are the first things to consider. Every region has a different set of laws about what renovations are allowed, what the process looks like and the permits required. As a general rule, permission to do renovations is easier in the rural areas, and difficult or impossible in the historical urban centers.

It's also important to remember that the rules are constantly changing. What was true a year ago could be completely different now.

Some renovations don't require permits if they are seen as regular maintenance on a property, and if they don't fundamentally change the exterior appearance or footprint of the property. Again, the rules on this vary from region to region.

There are companies that specialize in renovations. Hiring one of them to handle major renovation projects is recommended. They will know the local laws, understand the permitting process (and related "insider tricks") and have relationships with local contractors, such as tradespeople, surveyors and architects.

At the same time, you may find it useful to hire the services of a *geometra*. A geometra is sort of like a project manager and construction foreman rolled into one. They are your "go-to" person to handle all the aspects of the renovation project. If you don't speak Italian, a bi-lingual English/Italian geometra will be worth their weight in gold.

You can expect a renovation company to provide a complete plan with drawings that illustrate the work you'd like them to do. They will also be able to give you a rough timeline for the completion of the work and a cost estimate. The costs for renovation projects are quoted "per meter" so you'll have to do a little math to get the total cost.

**Property taxes**

Property taxes in Italy can seem complicated! When you are ready to make an offer on an Italian property, your notary can do the tax calculation for you so you know how much it will cost in the end. There are two tax values given to every property and they are linked for tax calculations.

One is the *rendita catastale,* which depends on the age, size and materials used to build the property. The rendita catastale will always be fixed unless a renovation project is completed and a new assessment is made.

The second tax value is the *valore catastale.* It is calculated based on a formula using the rendita catastale and is usually around 50-70% of the market value of a property. As you can imagine, there are frequent disputes about the true market value of a property when it comes to paying taxes. (There is an appeal process if you disagree with the assessed value).

A property's designation as a primary residence or secondary residence will also have an effect on the tax calculations. The tax is known as a registration tax (*imposta di registro).*

Tax when purchasing a primary residence: **9% of the valore catastale**

Tax when purchasing a primary residence *but you plan to apply for Italian residency in the next 18 months:* **2% of the valore catastale instead of 9%.** The 2% discount does not apply if the property is considered a "luxury" property.

(Note: If you declare you are going to become an Italian resident and don't do it within 18 months, you'll have to pay the 7% difference plus a 20% penalty when they catch you.)

Tax when purchasing a secondary residence: **9% of the valore catastale**

Tax when purchasing from a developer or custom builder: **4% of the purchase price** if it's a primary residence, **10% of the purchase price** if it's a secondary residence, or **22% of the purchase price** if the property is classified as a luxury property. These numbers only apply if the property is less than five years old.

Tax when purchasing agricultural land: **12% of the declared value of the land** (unless the land surrounds the house, in which case the calculation for the house can apply to both the land and the house).

## Annual property taxes

There is an annual tax paid to the local council in two installments (June and December). It is called the IMU tax. Residents do NOT have to pay this tax as long as their property is all classified as their primary residence. Non-residents pay according to a formula based on the rendita catastale and the formula is adjusted once a year by the local council. There are no notices sent for the IMU tax. You have to chase down the amount yourself twice a year.

Collected at the same time as the IMU, there is another tax called TASI. It is also calculated from the rendita catastale and pays for common usage things like road construction work and street lights. There are no notices sent for TASI, either.

Another tax is the garbage collection tax known as TARI. The rate depends on the number of people living in your residence and the size of the residence. There is a discount for those who have a secondary residence. Each property receives a separate bill (unlike the IMU).

## Taxes when selling

When selling a property in Italy, there are some taxes to consider if you have owned the property for under five years. Any profit from a sale of a property held for five years or less will be treated as capital gains and subject to income tax.

Costs related to renovation of a property can be used to offset any capital gains. It is important to keep records and invoices of any renovation work done to a property to prove how much you spent.

### Utilities

Whether you are renting or buying, you'll want to get your utilities set up before you move-in. It will be a nasty surprise if you arrive in your dream Italian home and there's no water or no electricity for you to use.

Water costs depend on where in Italy you live. Some regions have more water naturally available than others. The water bill comes twice a year and should be about the same amount every time, assuming you don't go over the standard billed amount (most households don't go over the limit). There are also special provisions and separate billing if you have a swimming pool, but it's easy to set it up.

Electricity is managed by the national power company. They provide a standard amount of power with flat-fee billing to each housing unit. You can request extra power if needed and you will receive a higher flat-fee bill. It's easy to go over the limit if you use power-hungry appliances like an air conditioner in the middle of the summer, so keep that in mind. After a few months of regular living, you should have a good handle on how much you'll pay every month.

If you're one of those old school types and would like a landline, that's fairly easy to do as well. Sometimes you can get a combination of a landline and home internet service. BE SURE TO CHECK your local area to see what internet service is available, if it's available at all! Some rural areas are not wired for high-speed internet to private homes.

As a stopgap, you can buy a hotspot and load it with a few gigabytes of data to get you started. There are a handful of cell phone companies with storefronts who will be able to help you. It won't be good for streaming videos, but you can do basic things with it until you get proper internet service if it's going to take a while (sometimes it takes a while).

## Healthcare

*The coronavirus pandemic of 2020 had some effect on the level of healthcare available in Italy. While returning to a "normal" system can be expected at some point, it would be wise to double-check the healthcare availability in the areas you are considering BEFORE you move there.*

Italy is a wonderfully healthy country. It consistently ranks in the top ten countries in the world for life expectancy at 84 years, and is always among the top three in Europe (with Switzerland and Spain). For comparison, the average life expectancy in the U.S. is 79 years (and declining every year).

The slow pace and low-stress lifestyle along with a healthy Mediterranean diet contribute to the longevity of the Italians. Their healthcare system is also great, ranking among the best in Europe.

The healthcare system is state-run and is inexpensive or free to residents. The system provides free emergency care to visitors from other countries as well. Most Italians maintain private insurance to give them more healthcare options when needed, but state-run healthcare is just fine in most circumstances. The cost of private health insurance is very reasonable in Italy.

## Schools and universities

There are five levels of the Italian education system: Kindergarten, primary school, lower secondary, upper secondary and university. The law states that children must attend school from age 6 until age 16. The school is state-sponsored, so there is no cost for students to attend. There are private schools available as well, although the public schools perform very well against them.

The Programme for International Student Assessment ranks school performance across various countries reported these findings in 2018:

*"Four regions and provinces in Italy sampled a sufficiently large number of schools and students to enable separate reporting of results. In reading, Trento and Bolzano scored at a similar level as Germany and Slovenia, and above the national average; Toscana scored close to the national average; and Sardegna scored below the national average, and at a similar level as Greece and Turkey. In mathematics, Trento and Bolzano scored*

*close to the top-performing European countries (Estonia, the Netherlands, Poland and Switzerland), and were outperformed only by the top-performing Asian countries and economies."*

Some documentation is required before a student can enroll in school. The documentation is the standard documentation required in modern countries such as proof of immunization, the appropriate residency document and a birth certificate.

Kindergarten (*asilo*) or nursery school is not required, but is available for children ages 3-6. Students usually enter primary school (*scuola elementare*) at age 6, although some exceptions are made for students who are 5.

The curriculum for all the schools covers the same core topics: Geography, history, mathematics, social studies, natural science, Italian, English and physical education.

After primary school, students attend two phases of secondary school. Lower secondary school (*scuola secondaria di primo grado*) lasts from ages 11 to 14, and upper secondary school (*scuola secondaria di secondo grado*) lasts from ages 14 to 19.

There are exams required at the end of each phase of secondary school, and success on those exams is required for admission to university.

The school days generally start at 8am and adjourn at 1pm. There are some variations to this schedule depending on the school as some schools are in session later than 1pm.

The university system in Italy is large and full of rich history. In fact, some of the oldest universities in the world can be found in Italy. Bachelor's, Master's and Doctorate programs are available in a variety of fields and most of the universities, colleges and academies are state supported.

## Banking in Italy

At some point during the relocation process, you'll need to transfer money from your home country's bank account to an Italian bank account. Taking some time to investigate the different international money transfer options could save you big money. The same goes for the regular fees in your bank account. Be patient here! It will pay to investigate some options before making a decision.

**Resident accounts versus non-resident accounts**

There are different fees for bank accounts depending on your residency status. Unsurprisingly, non-residents are charged much more to do their banking.

You will need to have an Italian bank account in order to perform basic tasks like paying your bills and your taxes.  The best advice is to start with a non-resident account as soon as you arrive, or see if there's a bank in your home country that offers "global" accounts that serve Italy to make money transfers easier.

You need a few specific items in order to open a non-resident bank account: Your passport, a *codice fiscale* (your Italian identification number) and a little cash to make an initial deposit.

The codice fiscale is free and easy to obtain. It's more of a national identification number than a "tax" number, although it is also used when you pay your taxes. It has many functions and you'll need it in order to sign-up for utilities, renting a flat or buying a motor vehicle. It is similar to a social security number in the U.S., or a national insurance number in the U.K.

## International money transfers

Transferring money to and from Italy will be easy for you if you have a bank that is familiar with international money transfers. (Hint: Most of the traditional big banks do a lousy job with international money transfers, and make them very expensive.)

Revolut is a great option. It's a newer online bank (launched in 2015) and they charge no fees for currency exchange or stock trading. They also have Visa debit cards and Mastercard prepaid cards available. Even if all you do with them is move money between different currencies or send money internationally, it's well worth having an account with them.

Some of the Italian online banks will serve your needs well as long as you are comfortable using your computer or smartphone. Everything is done online (including deposits...they are cashless banks), which is easy enough to manage once you get used to it. A few of the popular Italian online banks are Fineco and CheBanca. (Check their features against Revolut if you're going fully online...trust me on this one.)

Another option if you will maintain a U.S. address is to open a Schwab checking account and keep it active. The Schwab accounts have one advantage for frequent travelers that's hard to beat: You can use any ATM in the world to get cash in the local currency there, and Schwab will refund the fees you are charged by those ATMs.

That's right, they will refund the fees you were charged by the OTHER banks.

One thing to consider with your choice of bank (or banks) is whether or not you might want to apply for a mortgage in Italy someday. If a mortgage is on your agenda, it will be useful to have a banking relationship with one of the Italian banks in your area that has a mortgage division. You can always have a combination of an online bank (for currency exchange and foreign transactions) and a bank in your area for the purpose of obtaining a mortgage.

**Income tax**

Italy has some of the highest income tax rates in the world! They're consistently ranked in the top ten. You should have a solid understanding of what it means to move to Italy when it comes to your income, both earned in Italy and elsewhere.

Once you live in Italy for 183 days or more per year, you will be obligated to pay income taxes there. That includes your worldwide income on things like pensions, dividends or rental income.

If you live in Italy for fewer than 183 days per year, you only have to pay income tax on the money you made in Italy.

Rental income from properties in Italy earned by non-residents is taxable in Italy and uses the same brackets as residents. There is a lump sum deduction of 30% allowed for rental income for maintenance and repair costs that are expected as a landlord.

Selling a property held for five years or more will not result in any capital gains taxes. Selling a property held for five years or less results in the gains being taxed as regular income.

Income taxes are due by June 30th every year, although you can request a one-month delay for a penalty of .04%.

There are five tax brackets and different tax rates for each bracket. Below are the current brackets in euros.

- 0 - 15,000 = 23%
- 15,001 - 28,000 = 27%
- 28,001 - 55,000 = 38%
- 55,000 - 75,000 = 41%
- Over 75,000 = 43%

There is also an annual tax credit of €1840 available to all Italian taxpayers.

There are regional and municipal income taxes in addition to the national income tax. The regional taxes are up to 3.33% and the municipal taxes range from .01% to .09%.

## Starting a business in Italy

The mechanics for opening a business in Italy are similar to what you find in most other countries. You'll need to obtain a tax identification number, register for VAT, get a bank account and register your company with the applicable levels of government. It's wise to get professional help from a lawyer and accountant for all of these steps.

The corporate tax rate in Italy is 31.4% and the dividend tax rate is 20%. Business expenses and operating costs can be deducted from the total when figuring the taxable income, and you'll be responsible for regular filings and annual meetings. Again, you'll want to get help with this from an accountant.

**Starting a brick and mortar business**

Maybe your dream has been to move to the Italian countryside, buy a small vineyard and make your own wine and olive oil. I think that sounds like a splendid idea! Maybe your dream is to open an antique store and sell vintage items you find on your trips around Italy. Another splendid idea!

The process for opening a business that requires a physical location in Italy is similar to what you'll experience in most other countries. You'll have to navigate commercial zoning laws, local business registration, taxes, payroll, etc. Commercial leases have a higher degree of complexity (surprise, surprise) in Italy as well.

There's certainly nothing wrong with opening a brick and mortar business, but it shouldn't be confused with an entity that will print money for you without your participation.

Which brings us to...

**Starting an online business**

Assuming you're allowed to work while you're in Italy (or preparing to move to Italy), here's how to get started in only a few hours.

Be careful! Those living in Italy with the Elective Residency Visa (ERV) cannot work in Italy under any circumstances. That includes remote work, such as starting an online business as outlined below.

Real talk: Will you get caught if you are illegally working online? Maybe, maybe not. It is unlikely that the Italian police will knock on your door and demand to see what you are doing on your computer. BUT, you could be in for some serious trouble if you suddenly have an extra source of income to report on your tax return that didn't exist when you got your visa. Are you willing to risk your Italian residency status over this?

Why start an online business? Freedom, flexibility and money are the three reasons online entrepreneurs cite the most. They want to harvest money from the internet, make their own hours and work from whatever location suits them best that day.

Some people leave their day jobs to start an online business and very quickly end up broke! This happens when they go a little too heavy on the freedom and flexibility without enough focus on the making money part.

It's easy to get lost down rabbit holes of things that feel like work, but don't actually make you any money. Tasks like endlessly optimizing website designs or logos or complex sales funnels are common ways to burn days or weeks.

Don't be one of the people who is "getting ready to get ready" forever. You don't have an online business until it's making money for you. Until then, it's just a hobby.

Once you've decided it's time to get started, it's just a matter of putting the pieces together. People have lived before you and there's no need to reinvent the wheel.

**Step one: Figure out what you are going to sell**

You have a choice here. You can either find a product someone else has made and sell it on your website, or you can create a product of your own to sell on your website.

Creating your own product takes some time and energy, but the benefits are significant. It also gives you a degree of control that you don't have when you rely on someone else to create what you're selling.

For example, selling N95 face masks might seem like a great business these days. The people who had businesses selling these masks during the coronavirus pandemic ran into some challenges. The demand was through the roof! Great news, right?

Not quite.

There were some challenges filling orders from customers. The government was seizing any new shipments of N95 masks instead of letting them be shipped to their intended recipients.

To make it even more complicated, Facebook and Google banned all advertising for N95 masks (even from legitimate companies who had been advertising them for years). They had to do that because the scammers and price gougers showed up en masse when the coronavirus panic began. The problem was this policy ALSO harmed the legitimate sellers.

That's an extreme example, but you get the idea. You are always at risk if you are selling someone else's product. It's better to have your own product to sell, whether that's a physical product or a digital product.

Informational products are perfect items to sell on the internet. If your final product is an ebook or a course or an instructional video series, you can sell an infinite number of them after doing the work of creating it. Plus, it's easier to maintain a website than it is to manage physical inventory, production, shipping, returns, etc.

A common response here is, "But I don't have any special knowledge that anyone would pay for!"

You might be surprised.

I would argue that everybody has *something* of value they could teach others, no matter how obscure or unimportant or basic the knowledge might seem to you.

Some examples of informational products that sell well are cookbooks, Excel templates, personal finance guides and how-to courses for even the most basic subjects (think about how popular the *For Dummies* books have become...nothing is too basic). Somebody out there wants the knowledge you possess and it's your job to make it easy for them to find you on the internet.

The easiest informational products are the ones that don't take much or any technical skill to create. Which one of these do you think would be easiest for you? Pick one and start there.

- **Online courses**: A combination of text, audio and video content is the preferred delivery method these days.

There are some free Wordpress plugins (more on Wordpress later) that will do all the heavy lifting around the course structure and such. All you need to do is add the content. You can charge a flat fee per course

- **Ebooks**: Like the one you are reading right now! You can sell ebooks on your own website as well and many people do so with great success. I like the Kindle store because I can lean on Amazon's massive distribution reach. Ebooks don't need to be as robust as full-length paperback books and they can focus on the most obscure topics imaginable.

- **Membership websites**: This sort of business is a bit more involved because it requires some ongoing work in order for the value to be there for the members. The general idea is that you provide premium content of some sort that your users can access for a monthly membership fee. Many successful membership sites make some of their content available to everyone for free, and charge money for the premium content. These are good if you have some specific knowledge about a topic. Again, Wordpress has some free plugins that make the membership features easy to implement.

- **Online events or webinars**: These businesses are great alternatives to in-person events and seminars. People are willing to pay for high-quality content. Live events are one approach, and you can also record webinars and events to sell over and over in the future.

Once you have decided on your first product to create, it's time for the next step.

**Step two: Buy a domain name**

There are a bunch of places that will sell you a domain name. A domain name is the .com, .net, .info, etc. that people will use to find you and your website. The domain name for our main website is espatriati.com.

There are some important nuances to understand here. If at all possible, you want to find a domain with an extension that is a .com instead of a .net, .info, .news or any of the other dozens of options that have appeared over the past few years.

We went with .io for all of our domain names because we could keep it uniform across all of our web properties. There's no right or wrong here, but I would suggest not trying to be too clever with some of the bizarre extensions that are out there.

Also, try to keep the name short, simple, easy to spell and easy to pronounce. Assume that every visitor to your site will have no more than an eighth-grade education.

I understand many of the "good" .com names are taken. You can get some creative ideas by using a thesaurus if needed. A simple solution for many people is to buy your firstnamelastname.com, assuming you have a unique enough name that it isn't taken yet.

The domain registrar I recommend is GoDaddy. WARNING: GoDaddy will try to upsell you all sorts of things you don't need, like hosting, email, privacy (privacy is a maybe for you), etc. Decline all of it. Just pick your domain name and skip ahead to the checkout page. Also, you only have to register the domain for one year at a time, even though their default at check out will be five years. They are tricky like that.

**Step three: Get a quality hosting account**

Website files need a place to live and the companies that provide this service are called web hosts.

Buy this today: WP Engine is the best hosting provider I have found for the purpose of running an online business. They are the right combination of quality, price and AMAZING customer service. I've bothered them with so many random questions and they always find a way to help. (Check out website for a discount link for WP Engine)

This is especially important if you are not super technical. They have tutorials and live chat help for anything you'll need to do with your website.

They also make it easy to handle things like unexpected surges in website traffic, DDOS attacks and making regular backups of your site in case something goes wrong. You can also make changes in your website in "developer" mode, so the world won't see you experimenting with it. The customer support is top-notch as well (I like the Live Chat support function the best).

Once you have your hosting account, follow their instructions to connect your domain name from GoDaddy to your hosting account at WP Engine. They have tutorials and they make it easy for you.

**Step four: Install WordPress and get a proper WordPress theme**

This is my favorite step because it doesn't cost any money!

Wordpress is the framework that powers about one third of the websites in the world. It's FREE and easy to install through WP Engine. In fact, the "WP" in WP Engine comes from **W**ord**p**ress. They have all the support you'll need if you can't figure out how to do it yourself, but it's not hard. It should only take you a few minutes and a few clicks.

It *could* cost you money if you want to be super fancy, but there's no need to spend that money now. Save your money for a rainy day. Pick a free Wordpress theme from inside your Wordpress Dashboard (where you will make all the edits to your website). It's relatively easy and painless to upgrade to a paid theme later when your site is paying for itself, so don't sweat it.

Once you've installed WordPress, you will want to install a theme. A theme is what makes your website pretty. There are a gazillion free themes out there and a bunch of paid options, too. It's best to pick a free one for now and worry about updating to a paid one after you're more comfortable with the specific needs of your online business.

You'll find the free themes inside the WordPress dashboard once you have installed WordPress on your domain. You'll be prompted to create a username and password when you install WordPress and they'll email you login credentials. To install a theme, go to your WordPress dashboard, click on Appearance, then Themes. You'll see a bunch of free theme options in there. (Again, WP Engine has in-depth walkthrough articles and a responsive support team if you get stuck.)

All the themes focus on different features and they can do different things. WordPress is a very flexible framework and there are solutions for everything you can imagine. Plus, it doesn't require any coding or programming experience to work with it.

## Step five: Put a payment mechanism on your site

This step is also free. It will cost you nothing to create accounts with Paypal and Stripe. Go do that now.

Paypal is super simple and you probably already have an account with them. The easiest way to add payment options to your site for whatever you're selling is to add a Paypal button. You can follow the simple instructions inside your Paypal account for installing the button on your site.

Paypal will charge you a small percentage of your sales you make through the use of the Paypal button. You should also know that Paypal will take a few days to transfer money to your bank account when you're ready to collect your cash. It's mildly annoying, but you'll survive.

WARNING: Paypal has a nasty reputation if you make too many sales too fast. This is especially true if you have a new Paypal account and/or a new product you're selling with your Paypal button. Weird, right? I agree.

There are horror stories about people having their funds frozen by PayPal for weeks or months with no way to fix the problem (no phone number to call, emails and support messages are ignored). It's rare, but it happens. Paypal will probably work just fine forever for smaller projects, though. Consider yourself warned.

A better payment processing option once you have tested your product and it looks like people are ready to buy it is Stripe. Stripe takes a little more sophistication to implement on websites, but it's still on the easy end of technical skill.

Like Paypal, they allow you to establish an account for free and they take a small percentage of your sales that are processed through them. Stripe links to your bank account and automatically deposits your earnings on a regular basis. They have a great dashboard that allows you to track everything as well.

Stripe is growing by leaps and bounds. They continue to make improvements in functionality and ease of use. They also have a robust FAQ and tutorial section to help you get started with the more technical bits.

There are also merchant accounts available through most traditional banks. Payment processing through merchant accounts with a traditional bank should be avoided at all costs. They are clunky, horrendously expensive and they use outdated technology.

**Step six: Find customers**

"If you build it, they will come."

Hahaha. Nope.

You'll have to find a way to get customers to your site so they have a chance to buy your product. It's great when customers find your product through channels that don't cost you any money, like word-of-mouth, social media posts or search engine results. In the beginning, it's unlikely that enough customers will find you through the free channels, so you'll have to spend some money.

Google and Facebook are the big dogs when it comes to finding customers online through advertising. They both have advertising products that allow you to target people based on certain parameters. There are plenty of tutorials that will help you learn their systems.

I suggest setting a low budget and capping the daily amount of money you can spend on ads when you first start. If you don't put a cap on it, Google and Facebook will definitely take all of your money. You can learn and see what works with a small budget, then increase your budget later once you know the math and know what works.

**Step seven: Repeat as needed**

There's power in being focused. Pushing on only one product is the best approach until your product is reliably selling at a rate that is acceptable to you.

One of the benefits of informational products is that you should be able to automate most or all of the selling once you get the hang of it. Once that happens, you'll have some time on your hands to create another product.

Creating a natural extension or "sequel" of your first product is usually a good way to do it. You already have customers, an email list and you know how the ads perform in your category. There's no need to start over with something unfamiliar when you have so much leverage from your first product. For example, we have a few other "Move to ___" guides in the works for some other popular countries right now. And they have the added bonus of complementing our primary business!

One of my favorite success stories from this approach is Robert Kiyosaki with his Rich Dad series of books, courses and games. He built a brand around personal finance and created multiple products around the same theme. Regardless of what you think about the guy as a person, he was a master at building a large brand with informational products.

That's it! You should be good to go.

## Appendix 1: Preparation Checklist

Before you make the move to Italy, you'll want to make sure you have all your ducks in a row. Getting your visa is probably the biggest task you'll need to manage, but any international move has the potential to create hassles and headaches.

- You may wish to create your own checklist or spreadsheet for tracking and these items should give you a good start.
- Is your passport up to date, with at least six months left before it expires?
- Have you made a copy of your passport and visa documentation to carry with you?
- Have you emailed yourself a copy of your passport and visa documentation?
- Have you contacted your bank and credit card companies to let them know you'll be out of the country?
- Do you have proof of travel insurance? (Travel insurance coverage through credit cards doesn't count)
- Do you have enough euros to get you to your initial destination, or currency that can be exchanged for euros if there are no working ATMs at the airport?
- Have you downloaded all the appropriate travel apps?
- Have you downloaded an offline map on your phone with directions to your initial destination?
- Have you recently confirmed your hotel or short-term stay reservations?
- Have you recently confirmed any rental car or private driver reservations?

- Do you have a battery pack for charging your phone? Is it fully charged?
- Do you have an international phone plan, or a phone where you can add a local SIM card when you arrive?
- If traveling with pets, do you have the pet passport and immunization documentation?

## Appendix 2: Useful smartphone apps

One of the greatest parts about living in Italy is the easy access to so many wonderful destinations in Italy and other European countries. There's plenty to do and see in Italy, although a quick trip to Greece or Croatia will always be tempting.

In our always-connected world, you will want to have a fairly new smartphone that can run all the latest apps. Here are a few apps that will make your life easier when you're traveling in or around Italy.

**Omio** (formerly GoEuro) is a travel booking app. They partner with the providers of train, bus, ferry and airplane tickets. You can book tickets on the go and they have a mobile ticket function through the app so you don't have to mess with paper tickets.

**Hopper** is a flight booking app. It has a lovely interface that lets you pick two destinations and see the flight options months into the future in a calendar format. Each calendar date has a price on it and is coded with red (expensive for that route), yellow (average cost for that route) or green (cheap for that route). They allow you to set alerts for yourself if you want to watch a certain price and date that looks a little high and they will provide recommendations on whether you should book now or wait.

**Google Translate** is a free app that works like magic. You can easily type a word to translate into it and decide what language you'd like. Voila! That part is great, but the real magic is in the live camera translation function. Imagine being in a restaurant and they only have menus in Italian, but you don't speak Italian. No problem! Fire up your Google Translate app and push the camera icon. The app will TRANSLATE THE MENU IN ENGLISH IN REAL TIME. You really have to see it to believe it. They keep adding more support such as static photo translation and voice translation support.

**Speak & Translate** has saved me a few times over the years. Google has added some similar functionality as well. The way this works is you speak whatever you want to say in your normal English voice and in a few seconds, it will recite it back in Italian (or whatever other language you choose). This is very handy when you're trying to communicate something in another language that requires some explanation. It costs a few euros to buy this app, but it's well worth it.

**Duolingo** is a great language learning app. It will help you get a head start on your Italian, and dozens of other languages. They have both free and paid versions. Start with the free version and see how far you get before you upgrade.

**Ridesharing apps** are a must-have these days. Uber is one of the biggest and most popular in the world. One of the most common ways people get ripped-off when traveling is by taxi drivers (which is why Uber got started in the first place). Taxi drivers know they have suckers in the car who don't know the customary pricing or most direct routes to their destinations. Uber may or may not be legal in Italy by the time you read this because taxi companies work very hard to keep Uber out of town.

*As of the time of this writing (April 2020), the only version of Uber that's available in Italy is when you schedule a car in advance. It's the same rules for taxis in Italy—you have to call one or go to a taxi stand. They are not allowed to pick up people hailing them on the streets.*

**TripAdvisor** is a good forum for all things travel, including restaurants, activities and local tips. You can also ask questions on the forum if you can't find an answer there.

**Yelp** is great for reading reviews from customers of shops, restaurants, bars and more! It isn't available in every country, though. Pro tip: You will also have to learn to read between the lines when reading restaurant reviews written by Americans who were on vacation. They have a tendency to criticize the level of service even if everything else was perfect and dock the restaurants a few stars. (They are used to servers working hard for tips and prompt service...not European service).

**HotelTonight:** Book same-day hotels at steep discounts. Hotels put their excess inventory on the HotelTonight app. Bonus! If you use the code JSTERLING3 when you sign up, you get $25 off your first booking.

Here are a few more to consider, without the colorful descriptions:

**Trenìt:** Train timetable and booking app

**Eat Italy:** A food guide for foodies

**Rick Steves:** Audio files to guide you on your trips around Europe

**Airbnb:** Great for short-term housing needs, and also their new "Experiences" section

**TripIt:** Consolidates all of your travel itineraries in one place

**WifiMapper:** Find the closest wifi to you

Thank you for reading our guide. If there is something that is unclear or missing, please email us info@espatriati.com and we will do our best to help you. We want this guide to be a five-star experience and we will make updates from time to time.

If you enjoyed the guide, we appreciate all the nice reviews on Amazon. They really help! A few sentences will work just fine.

*If you would like to be notified of future "Move to _____" country guides, please visit www.espatriati.com and sign-up for our regular mailing list. We have a few in the works that will be released soon!*

Made in United States
Troutdale, OR
10/25/2024

24115104R00046